Aa Word Tracing

Direction: Trace the words for each picture.

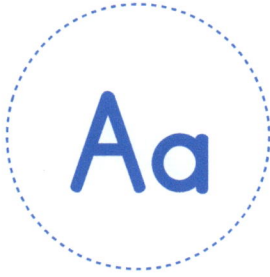

acorn

albatross

anchor

ant

Direction: Trace the words for each picture.

butterfly

boat

balloon

banana

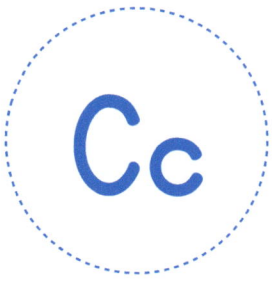

Cc Word Tracing

Direction: Trace the words for each picture.

cat

carrot

cake

candy

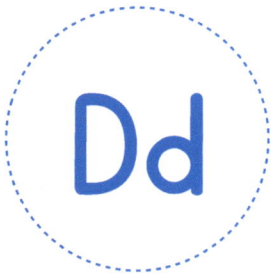

Word Tracing

Direction: Trace the words for each picture.

duck

drum

dolphin

donut

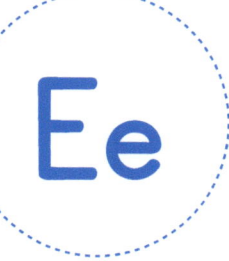

Ee Word Tracing

Direction: Trace the words for each picture.

elephant

eggplant

earth

eagle

Direction: Trace the words for each picture.

flower

frog

fan

fire

Word Tracing

Direction: Trace the words for each picture.

grapes

giraffe

guitar

girl

Word Tracing

Direction: Trace the words for each picture.

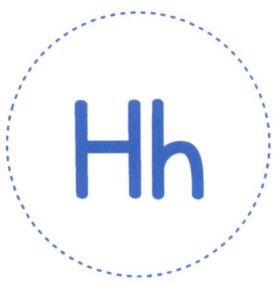 house

 hat

 heart

 hand

Word Tracing

Direction: Trace the words for each picture.

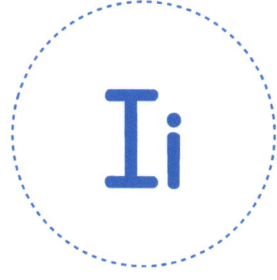

insect

ice cream

island

igloo

Jj

Word Tracing

Direction: Trace the words for each picture.

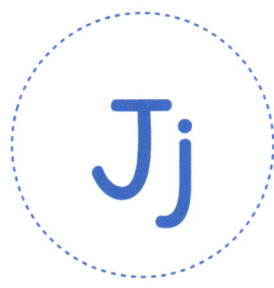

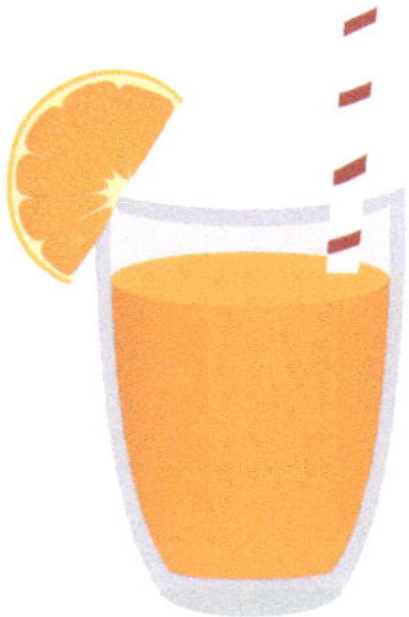

juice

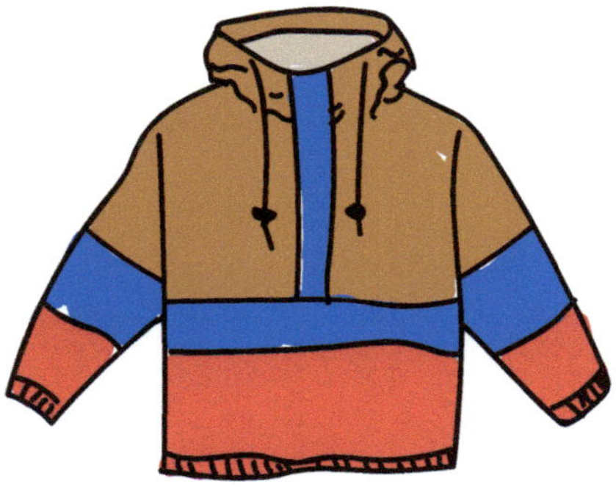

jacket

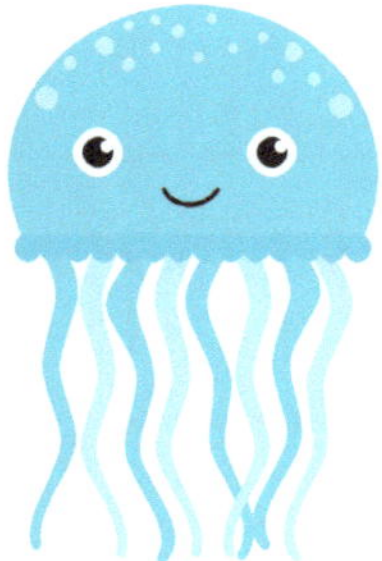

jellyfish

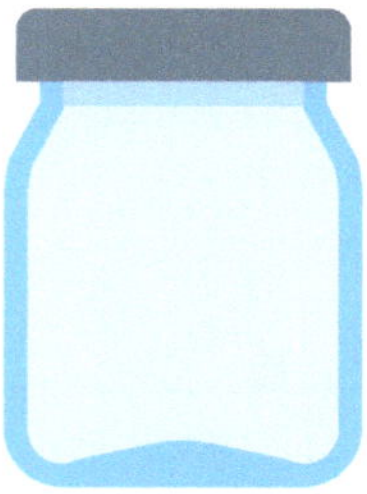

jar

Kk Word Tracing

Direction: Trace the words for each picture.

kite

kangaroo

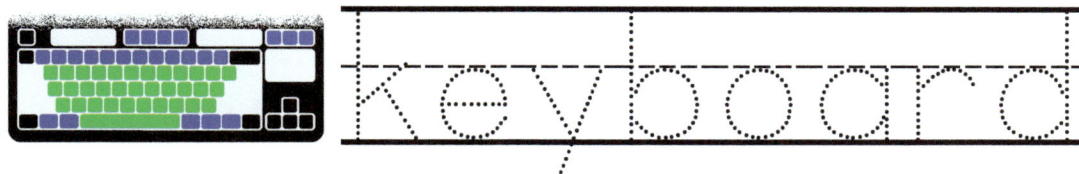

keyboard

koala

Trace the numbers and color the pictures.

1

one

one one one

one one one

Trace the numbers and color the pictures.

2

two

2 2 2 2 2

2 2 2 2 2

two two two

two two two

Trace the numbers and color the pictures.

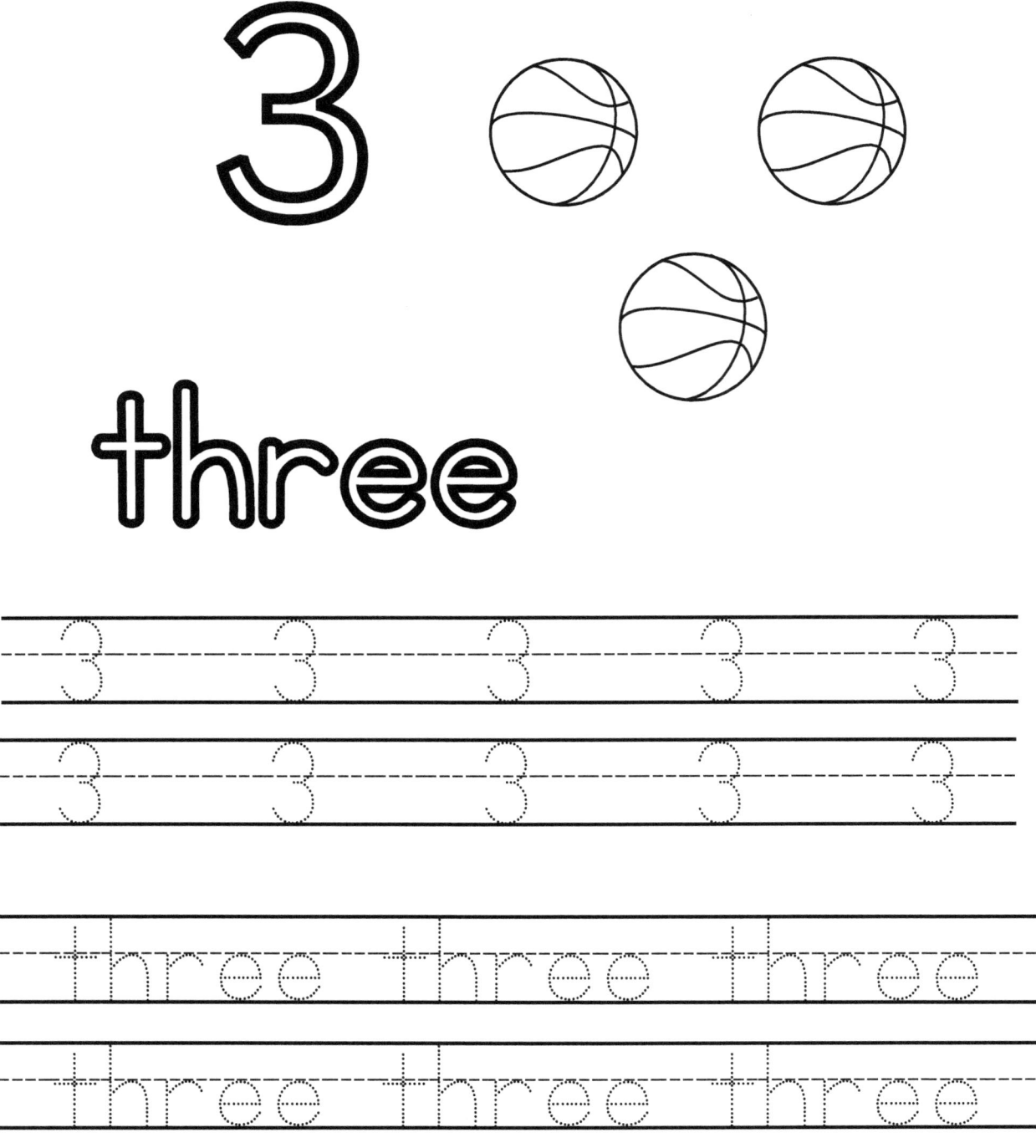

3

three

3 3 3 3 3

3 3 3 3 3

three three three

three three three

Trace the numbers and color the pictures.

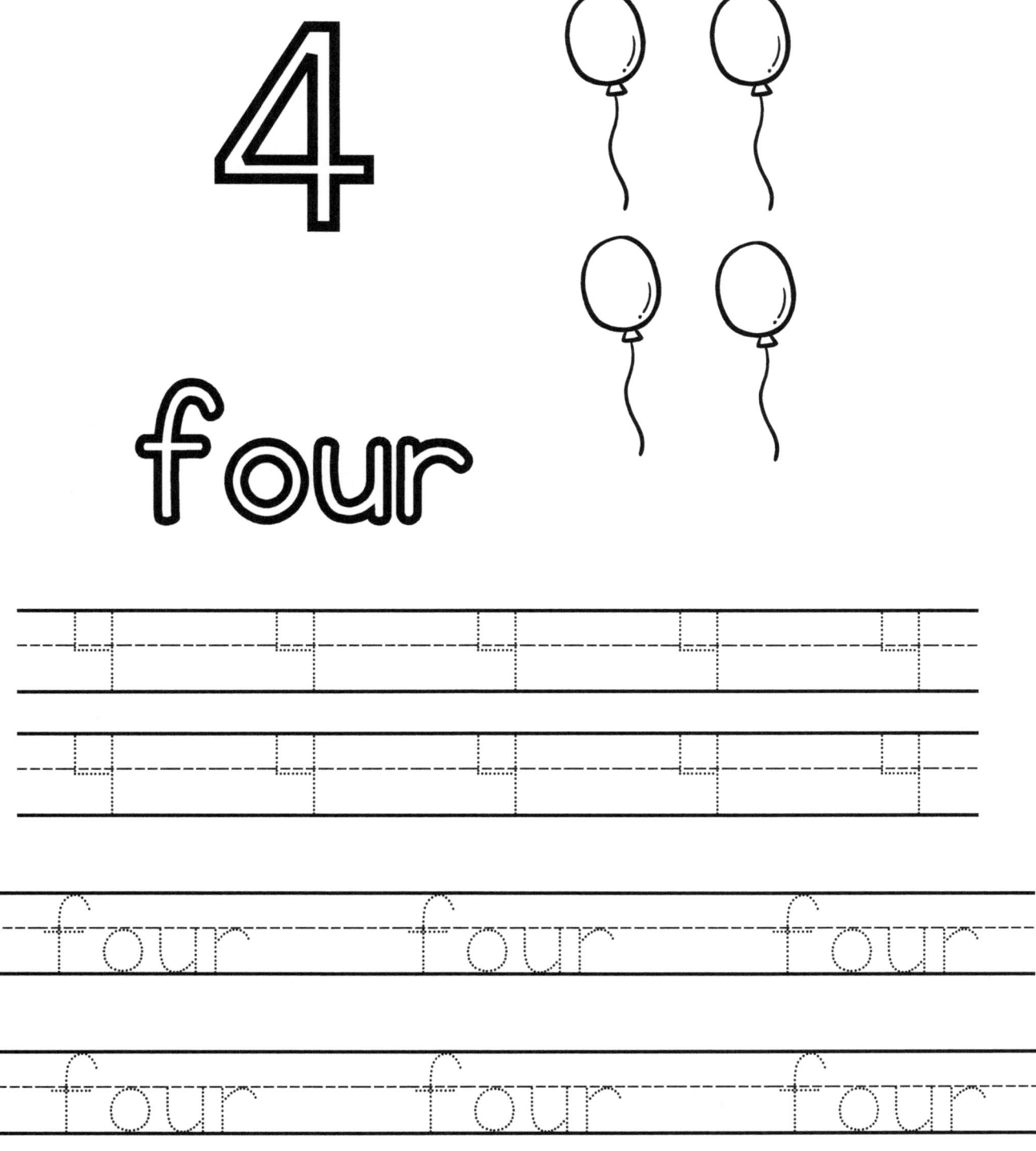

4

four

4   4   4   4   4

4   4   4   4   4

four   four   four

four   four   four

Trace the numbers and color the pictures.

5

five

5 5 5 5 5

5 5 5 5 5

five five five

five five five

Ladder Climbers Publishing

Trace the numbers and color the pictures.

six

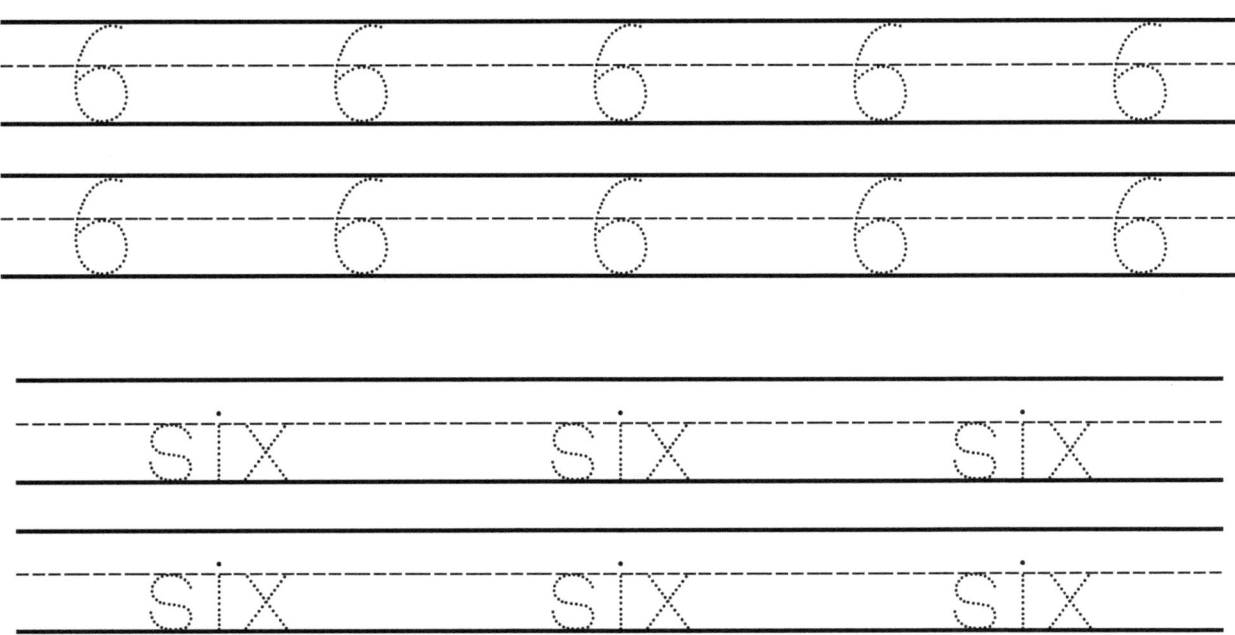

Ladder Climbers Publishing

Trace the numbers and color the pictures.

7

seven

7 7 7 7 7 7

7 7 7 7 7 7

seven seven seven

seven seven seven

Trace the numbers and color the pictures.

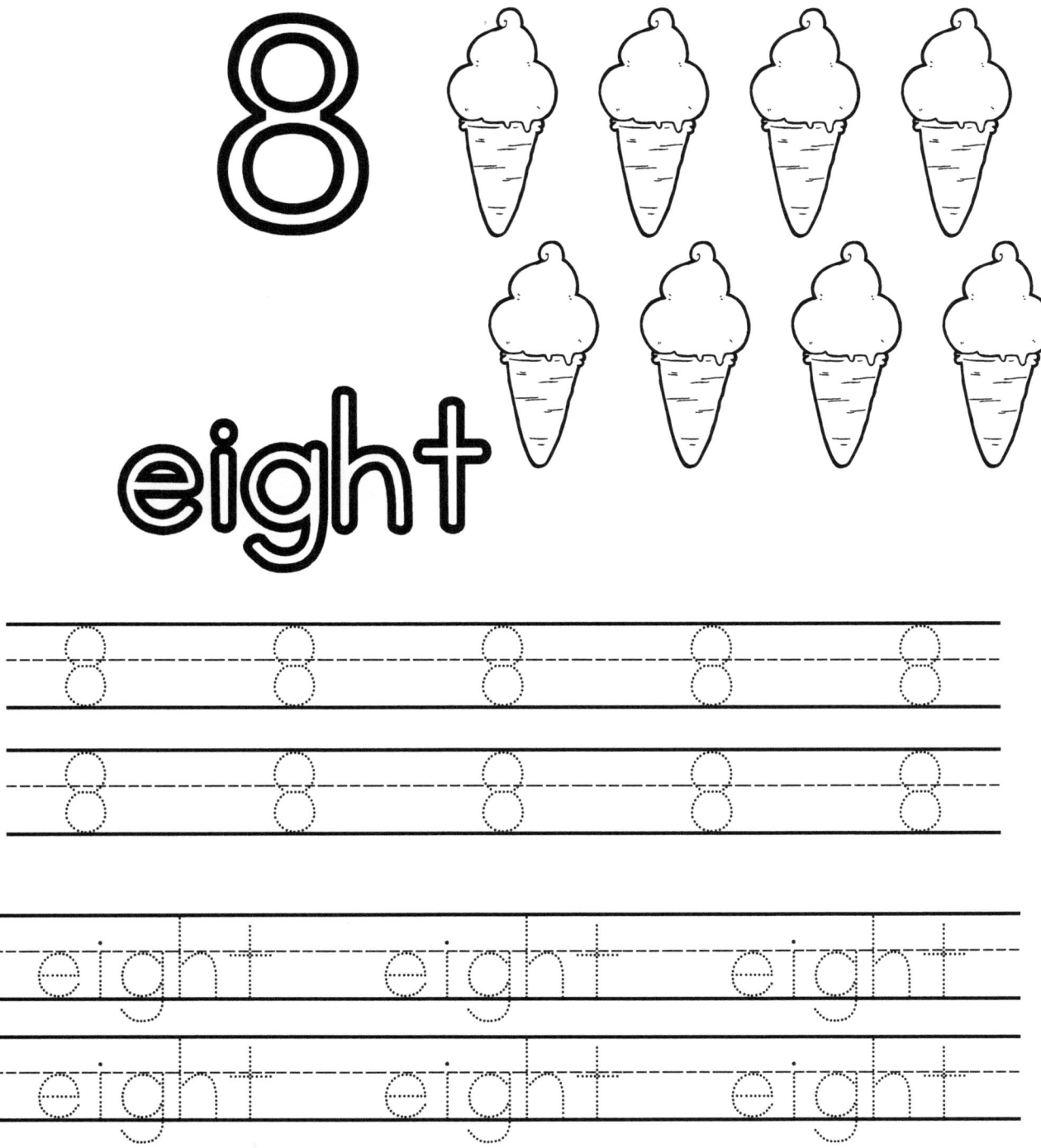

Trace the numbers and color the pictures.

9

nine

q q q q q

q q q q q

nine nine nine

nine nine nine

Trace the numbers and color the pictures.

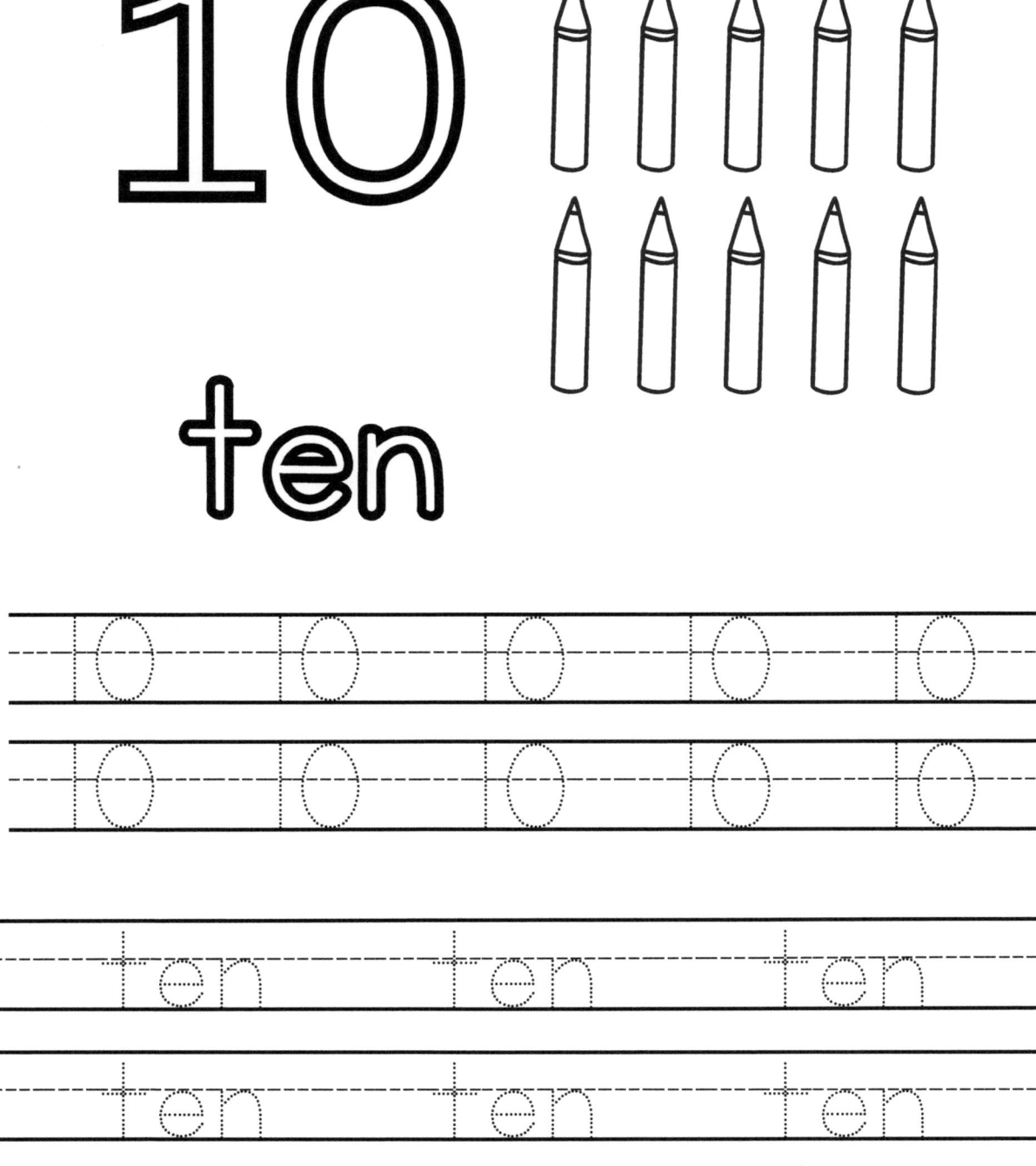